Tackling Numeracy Issues

Book 3

Fractions, Decimals, Percentages, Ratio and Proportion

Key Stage 2
Years 5 and 6

Caroline Clissold

The *Questions* Publishing Company Limited
Birmingham
2002

The Questions Publishing Company Limited
Leonard House, 321 Bradford Street, Digbeth, Birmingham B5 6ET

First published in 2002

ISBN: 1-84190-047-8

Design by Al Stewart
Cover by Martin Cater and incidental illustrations by John Minett

Printed in the UK

Also available from The Questions Publishing Company Limited:

Book 1 *Fractions and Decimals, Key Stage 1*
ISBN: 1-84190-079-6

Book 2 *Fractions, Decimals and Percentages, Key Stage 2*
ISBN: 1-84190-047-8

Book 4 Solving Maths Word Problems
ISBN: 1-84190-052-4

Book 5 *Improving the Plenary Session, Key Stage 1, Years 1 and 2*
ISBN: 1-84190-053-2

Book 6 *Improving the Plenary Session, Key Stage 2, Years 3 and 4*
ISBN: 1-84190-077-X

Book 7 *Improving the Plenary Session, Key Stage 2, Years 5 and 6*
ISBN: 1-84190-078-8

Contents

Definitions

Fraction
A part of something split into equal parts, made up of a numerator and denominator, for example ¼.

Decimal
A number like 0.2 and 3.25. They are 'part numbers', because they include amounts that are less than one.

Percentage
A special fraction that has a denominator of 100, like $^{67}/_{100}$. We write this as 67%. Per cent means 'for every hundred'.

Ratio
The relationship between two quantities, for example if we used 100 ml of juice and 300 ml of water to make a drink, the ratio would be 1:3 – one part of juice for every three parts of water.

Proportion
The relationship between measures or quantities, for example if there were ten dogs, three were wearing collars, the proportion wearing collars would be three in every ten. This can be expressed as a fraction or percentage, i.e. $^{3}/_{10}$ or 30%.

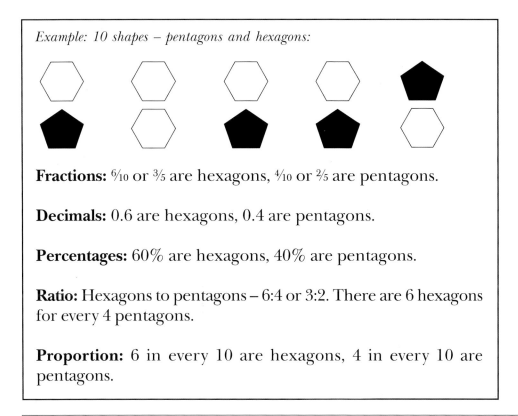

Example: 10 shapes – pentagons and hexagons:

Fractions: $^{6}/_{10}$ or $^{3}/_{5}$ are hexagons, $^{4}/_{10}$ or $^{2}/_{5}$ are pentagons.

Decimals: 0.6 are hexagons, 0.4 are pentagons.

Percentages: 60% are hexagons, 40% are pentagons.

Ratio: Hexagons to pentagons – 6:4 or 3:2. There are 6 hexagons for every 4 pentagons.

Proportion: 6 in every 10 are hexagons, 4 in every 10 are pentagons.

Introduction

The concepts of fractions, decimals, percentages, ratio and proportion are hard for children to understand. It is vital therefore that the foundations are laid for them early in their education and that these are secure within them, so that they can be built upon later.

In the **Foundation Stages**, which include Reception, children will develop an early experience of numbers through activities in real life or role-play contexts. They are introduced to the idea of half – half full, half past 10, share out the cubes so that you have half each, fold the paper in half, and so on. Initially, they will understand this as a part of something, rather than one of two equal parts. This will need reinforcement regularly, in order to help them to remember and begin to build that initial foundation block of fraction understanding.

Key Stage 1 progresses on from this, focusing on simple fractions (halves and quarters), decimals in the context of money, and early ideas of ratio and proportion.

In **Key Stage 2**, the ideas should be developed in a wide range of contexts, including practical work on money, measurement and problem solving.

Progression

The progression for this topic begins in the Early Years, but becomes a formal progression in Year 2. This is a very important year for the introduction of fractions as it provides the basis for future scaffolding. It is imperative that the children are given time for practical exploration of halves and quarters and are not rushed on too quickly to more complex fraction work.

It is important that children fully understand these concepts:

o halves and quarters of shapes and small numbers of objects;
o the equivalences between them, i.e. two halves and four quarters are both the same as a whole, one half and two quarters are the same.

Once this foundation has truly been built, the rest should come more easily. The children should not be moved on until a firm understanding of this initial concept has been achieved. At each stage in the children's progression through this topic it is important only to move on to the next step when they are ready.

Making links

Children and many adults often do not appreciate that fractions, decimals and percentages are equivalent ways of writing the same quantity and that fractions, decimals, percentages, ratio and proportion (FDPRP) are different ways of expressing related ideas.

To be an effective teacher of this topic, it is important to have a knowledge and awareness of the conceptual connections between these five ideas.

To develop into competent mathematicians, children need to understand the place of fractions and decimals in our number system; they need to be able to use the language of fractions confidently.

Many children have difficulty recognising equivalences in fractions, which is why it is very important to make these links at the earliest opportunity and regularly after that, beginning in Year 2 with quarters, halves and wholes.

Children also have difficulty making the links between fractions, decimals and percentages. Take every opportunity to help children appreciate these connections. Provide a range of practical contexts for children to explore and use FDPRP. Ensure that children see FDPRP expressed in different ways and appreciate that the representations are of related ideas.

To develop the children's understanding and the connections between these ideas, they need good experience of them in varied practical contexts and the links need to be explicit. Include, in your teaching, a wide range of opportunities to solve problems involving FDPRP in real life contexts, money and measures.

When teaching FDPRP you need to be aware of the lines of progression in the numeracy framework and the aspects that children are likely to find difficult.

Common misconceptions

○ Children are not always aware that fractions can be used in two ways: as a proportion of something, for example ¼ of £8; and as a fixed mark, for example ½ is midway between 0 and 1.

○ Many children do not recognise that fractions can be represented in several ways, for example:

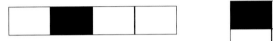 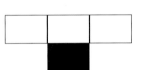

They need plenty of opportunities to experience this.

○ Some children take a while to fully understand that when a whole is divided into fractions, each fraction is an equal part. For example, children may think that the following diagram shows fifths because there are five parts. They need to realise that because the parts are not equal, they are not fifths.

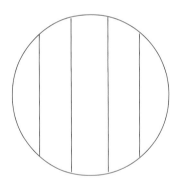

○ Many children believe that the bigger the denominators that make up the fraction, the bigger the fraction is, for example ⅕ is a larger fraction than ⅓.

○ Because multiplication makes numbers larger, many children think that this will happen to fractions – but in fact, multiplying a whole number by a fraction makes the answer smaller.

○ Some children think that decimal numbers are larger than whole numbers because there are more digits, for example 2.145 is larger than 3.

Correct terms and notation

Numerator

The top number in a fraction, which shows us how many parts of something we have.

Denominator

The bottom number of a fraction, which shows us how many equal parts the whole has been divided into.

Proper fraction

A fraction where the numerator is less than the denominator.

Improper fraction

A fraction where the numerator is larger than the denominator.

Mixed number

A whole number with a proper fraction beside it, for example 3 ¼.

Vulgar fraction

The family word for all fractions.

Decimal fraction

The proper word for what we call a decimal.

Decimal point

This separates the whole numbers from the part numbers that are less than one.

Decimal place

The number of decimal places is the number of digits to the right of the decimal point, for example 12.75 has two decimal places.

Fractions

To develop an understanding of fractions, children must be given experiences that enable them to discover that fractions:

- are equal parts of a whole and that the number of parts gives the fraction its name;
- have equivalences and what these are;
- can be combined, compared, ordered and taken apart, and how this happens;
- are not ordinal numbers, i.e. an eighth is one part of a whole divided into eight, not the eighth position;
- of the same type are equal even if they appear to be different sizes, for example ½ of 24 = 12, ½ of 4 = 2, both are halves, it is the quantity that is different.

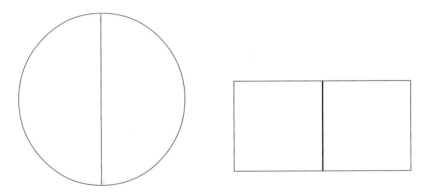

Children need to develop an understanding of the links between division and fractions, that if the numerator is divided by the denominator it will be converted into a decimal fraction and can sometimes be easier to understand or calculate as one. They need to develop their understanding of fraction vocabulary and be able to use this to discuss their work and record it.

This will all lead to a greater understanding of the addition, subtraction, multiplication and division of fractions, which will be important to them when they go to secondary school.

Decimal fractions

Initially, to help promote children's understanding, decimals are taught through money and measurement. Gradually children need to build up an understanding of decimals as parts of any whole numbers.

Work needs to be done on the place value of decimals, so that the children understand the concept of tenths being ten times smaller than a single digit unit and hundredths being one hundred times smaller. Practical activities involving the children are helpful, for example prepare some digit cards on A4 paper; include a decimal point. Give one child the decimal point, and give four others the digit cards. Ask them to make the largest number they can (by standing in the correct order), maybe 7532. Then ask them to divide it by 10, 100, multiply by 10, and so on. The children will need to place themselves around the decimal point. Make up new numbers from those digits and repeat the exercise.

When children are calculating mentally, they may use a strategy, for instance pretending the number is an amount of money, or pretending it is a whole number and then replacing the decimal point. This is acceptable as an efficient method of calculation, providing they understand the place value of the original number.

Addition, subtraction, multiplication and division of decimals come as a natural progression. If the children do not have a strong grasp of the concept of decimal fractions then they will not be experienced enough to tackle this next step. They will need to move back a stage in the progression and concentrate on becoming totally confident with decimals.

Percentages

Percentages are fractions whose denominator is 100, for example $^{12}/_{100}$. It is important that the children understand this concept and initially work with percentages as amounts out of 100. It is important to link common fractions with percentages, for example ½ = 50%, ¼ = 25%. This should be done visually, with you as the teacher modelling this experience. Later on in this book there is an excellent example of how this can be done (see page 17). When the children have grasped this, move on to amounts out of 50 (by halving) and 200 (by doubling).

Next they need to be given experiences to develop an understanding of the relationship between fractions, decimals and percentages and the ability to convert from one to the other.

Common equivalences

These need teaching, so that the children learn them as facts:

½ = 0.5 = 50%

¼ = 0.25 = 25%

¾ = 0.75 = 75%

⅛ = 0.125 = 12½ %

⅒ = 0.1 = 10%

Many other facts can be worked out from this knowledge.

Ratio and proportion

Ratio and proportion appear in the curriculum at Year 4. The children need very practical ways to experience them, for example investigating the proportions of colours used when mixing paints and practising ratio when exploring the scales on maps.

They need to understand that these are quantities that have a constant rule.

QCA demands

QCA's analysis of 1999 KS2 tests found that to raise standards, more effective teaching is needed in these areas:

- reducing fractions to their lowest form;
- ordering a set of mixed numbers;
- using decimal notation for tenths and hundredths;
- relating fractions to their decimal representations;
- finding simple percentages of small whole number quantities.

It also states that:

'Teachers should give a greater emphasis to place value when teaching decimals and not rely on money and measure context. Decimal place value has to be mastered in its own right.'

And:

'Children do not understand percentage as the number of parts per hundred, for example that 40% means 40 parts per hundred parts and that this can be written as the fraction $\frac{40}{100}$ or $\frac{4}{10}$ or $\frac{2}{5}$.'

One of the aims of this book is to help you, as the teacher, to teach these areas of fractions, decimals and percentages more effectively. It provides follow-up activities that will help to reinforce your teaching and enable the children to understand these concepts and to be able to make use of them in future 'real life' situations.

Excellent teaching

The following suggestions offer some thoughts to have in mind while you plan.

Excellent teaching occurs when:

- lessons are kept simple and there are effective, but not too many, resources;
- there is space for direct teaching;
- there is correct use of vocabulary and phrasing from both teacher and child;
- there is questioning, and answers are given, in sentences;
- modelling and demonstrating are done using the equipment the children are expected to use;
- step-by-step teaching is employed;
- objectives are shared between teacher and children;
- there are high expectations;
- planning has been well thought out.

The activities in this book are designed to help you teach fractions, decimals, percentages, ratio and proportion effectively. Most of the ideas can be adapted to use in different year groups and with different abilities of children.

The following is the National Numeracy Strategy's progression through fractions, decimals, percentages, ratio and proportion. Year 2 to Year 6 has been included to provide an overview of the whole progression throughout this topic. Although you may be responsible for one particular year group it is important to have a sense of the requirements of children at each step of Key Stage 2. This will help you to understand how children develop their knowledge of these concepts. The most important point to remember is that as a teacher you must ensure that the children in your class have a complete and full understanding of an objective before you move them on.

Progression through fractions, decimals, percentages, ratio and proportion

Year 2

- Begin to recognise and find one half and one quarter of shapes and numbers of objects.
- Begin to recognise that two halves or four quarters make one whole and that two quarters and one half are equivalent.

Year 3

- Recognise unit fractions such as ½, ⅓, ¼, ⅕, ⅒, and use them to find fractions of shapes and numbers.
- Begin to recognise simple fractions that are several parts of a whole, such as ¾, ⅔ or ³⁄₁₀.
- Begin to recognise simple equivalent fractions: for example, five tenths and one half, five fifths and one whole.
- Compare familiar fractions: for example, know that on the number line one half lies between one quarter and three quarters.
- Estimate a simple fraction.

Year 4

- Use fraction notation.
- Recognise simple fractions that are several parts of a whole, such as ⅔ or ⅝, and mixed numbers, such as 5¾.
- Recognise the equivalence of simple fractions (for example, fractions equivalent to ½, ¼ or ¾).
- Identify two simple fractions with a total of 1, for example ³⁄₁₀ and ⁷⁄₁₀.
- Order simple fractions: for example, decide whether fractions such as ⅜ or ⁷⁄₁₀ are greater or less than one half.
- Begin to relate fractions to division and find simple fractions such as ½, ⅓, ¼, ⅕, ⅒ of numbers or quantities. Find fractions such as ⅔, ¾, ⅗, ⁷⁄₁₀ of shapes.
- Begin to use ideas of simple proportion: for example, one for every . . . and one in every . . .

- Understand decimal notation and place value for tenths and hundredths, and use it in context: for example, order amounts of money; convert a sum of money such as £13.25 to pence, or a length such as 125cm to metres; round a sum of money to the nearest pound.
- Recognise the equivalence between the decimal and the fraction forms of one half and one quarter, and tenths such as 0.3.

Year 5

- Use fraction notation, including mixed numbers and the vocabulary numerator and denominator.
- Change an improper fraction into a mixed number, for example change $^{13}/_{10}$ to $1^{3}/_{10}$.
- Recognise when two simple fractions are equivalent, including relating hundredths to tenths, for example $^{70}/_{100} = ^{7}/_{10}$.
- Order a set of fractions such as 2, $2^{3}/_{4}$, $1^{3}/_{4}$, $2^{1}/_{2}$, and position them on a number line.
- Relate fractions to division, and use division to find simple fractions, including tenths and hundredths, of numbers and quantities, for example $^{3}/_{4}$ of 12, $^{1}/_{10}$ of 50, $^{1}/_{100}$ of £3.
- Solve simple problems using ideas of ratio and proportion (one for every . . . one in every . . .).
- Use decimal notation for tenths and hundredths.
- Know what each digit represents in a number with two decimal places.
- Order a set of numbers or measurements with the same number of decimal places.
- Round a number with one or two decimal places to the nearest integer.
- Relate fractions to their decimal representations, for example $^{1}/_{2} = 0.5$, $^{1}/_{4} = 0.25$, $^{3}/_{4} = 0.75$, and tenths and hundredths such as $^{7}/_{10} = 0.7$, $^{27}/_{100} = 0.27$.
- Begin to understand percentage as the number of parts in every 100, and find simple percentages of whole-number quantities, for example 25% of £8.
- Express one half, one quarter, three quarters and tenths and hundredths, as percentages, for example $^{3}/_{4} = 75\%$.

Year 6

○ Change a fraction such as $^{33}/_{8}$ to the equivalent mixed number $4^{1}/_{8}$ and vice versa.

○ Recognise relationships between fractions, for example $^{1}/_{10}$ is ten times $^{1}/_{100}$, and $^{1}/_{16}$ is half of $^{1}/_{8}$.

○ Reduce a fraction to its simplest form by cancelling common factors in the numerator and denominator.

○ Order fractions such as $^{2}/_{3}$, $^{3}/_{4}$, and $^{5}/_{6}$ by converting them to fractions with a common denominator and position them on a number line.

○ Use a fraction (including tenths and hundredths) as an operator to find fractions of numbers or quantities, for example $^{5}/_{8}$ of 32, $^{7}/_{10}$ of 40, $^{8}/_{100}$ of 400cm.

○ Solve simple problems involving ratio and proportion.

○ Use decimal notation for tenths and hundredths in calculations, and tenths, hundredths and thousandths when recording measurements.

○ Know what each digit represents in a number with up to three decimal places.

○ Give a decimal fraction lying between two others, for example between 3.4 and 3.5.

○ Order a mixed set of numbers or measurements with up to three decimal places.

○ Round a number with two decimal places to the nearest tenth or whole number.

○ Recognise the equivalence between the decimal and fraction forms of one half, one quarter, one eighth and tenths, hundredths and thousandths, for example $^{700}/_{1000} = {}^{70}/_{100} = {}^{7}/_{10} = 0.7$.

○ Begin to convert a fraction to a decimal using division.

○ Understand percentages as the number of parts in every 100. Express simple fractions such as one half, one quarter, three quarters, one third, two thirds and tenths and hundredths as percentages, for example know that $^{1}/_{3} = 33 \frac{1}{3}\%$.

○ Find simple percentages of small whole-number quantities, for example find 10% of £500, then 20%, 40% and 80% by doubling.

Ready reference table: Book 3

Chapter	Numeracy Strategy	National Curriculum
1 Play your cards right	Years 5 and 6	Key Stage 2/2d Key Stage 2/2e Key Stage 2/2f Key Stage 2/2i
2 Cover them up	Years 5 and 6	Key Stage 2/2d Key Stage 2/2e Key Stage 2/2f Key Stage 2/2i
3 Percentage squares	Years 5 and 6	Key Stage 2/2f
4 Percentage game	Years 5 and 6	Key Stage 2/2f
5 Improper fractions	Years 5 and 6	Key Stage 2/2d Key Stage 2/2e
6 Fractions to decimals	Years 5 and 6	Key Stage 2/2i
7 Paint ratios	Years 5 and 6	Key Stage 2/2h
8 Map reading	Years 5 and 6	Key Stage 2/2h
9 Ratios and heights	Years 5 and 6	Key Stage 2/2h
10 My body	Years 5 and 6	Key Stage 2/2h

Chapter 1

Play your cards right

A fun game to play with groups of children or the whole class, maybe as part of your plenary session.

Preparation
Enlarge and copy the photocopiable sheets 1 and 2 onto card. Make sure that they are big enough for the whole class to see.

Activity
Prepare between 20 to 30 fraction, decimal and percentage cards from 0 to 1. Mix them up and put in a pile. Ask someone to take a card. Stick this to the board or stand it up where it can be seen. The children need to predict whether the next card is going to be higher or lower than the one showing. The next card is picked and shown to the class. If it agrees with the prediction made by the majority of the class, it is placed beside the last card. If not start again. The aim is to get five cards in a row.

While playing make sure you always ask the children appropriate questions such as "How much bigger is this card?", "What percentage is this fraction equivalent to?", and so on.

Example 1

1.
$$\frac{3}{4}$$

The majority of the class predict that the next card will be higher.

2.
0.9

They are correct. Ask "Why is this bigger?" "What is ¾ as a decimal?"

The majority of the class predict that the next card will be lower.

3.
90%

They are wrong. Ask why and begin the game again.

Example 2

1.

0.1

The majority of the class predict that the next card will be higher.

2.

³⁄₁₀

They are correct. Ask "Why is this bigger?" "What is 0.1 as a fraction?"

The majority of the class predict that the next card will be higher.

3.

75%

They are correct. Why? Their next prediction is lower.

4.

⁴⁄₆

Correct. Their next prediction is lower again. They are correct. Game over.

5.

0.25

Key questions

- How much bigger/smaller is this card?
- What percentage is this fraction equivalent to?
- What is the difference between this amount and the last one?
- What is this as a decimal?
- How do you know that this is bigger or smaller?
- Why do you think that the next card will be bigger or smaller?
- Why is it difficult to predict this?

Photocopiable Sheet 1
Play your cards right A

$\frac{1}{5}$	$\frac{2}{5}$	$\frac{3}{5}$
$\frac{1}{2}$	$\frac{1}{3}$	$\frac{1}{4}$
$\frac{3}{4}$	$\frac{2}{6}$	$\frac{1}{8}$
$\frac{7}{8}$	$\frac{3}{10}$	$\frac{9}{10}$
0.1	0.2	0.3

Photocopiable Sheet 2
Play your cards right B

0.4	0.5	0.6
0.25	0.75	0.125
0.9	25%	30%
50%	75%	60%
80%	90%	95%

Chapter 2

Cover them up

This is another game that is ideal for an oral and mental starter or plenary session as it can be played with the whole class. Alternatively, smaller groups could play it during the main part of the lesson.

Preparation
You will need:

○ a copy of the cover up grid appropriate to your children (see photocopiable sheets 3 and 4).

○ 16 counters or small pieces of paper per player.

Activity
Ask the children to cover up certain numbers on their grid by answering your questions, for example cover up any numbers that are equivalent to ½, cover up some numbers that total 20%.

50%	¼	0.4	10%
5%	2/5	7/8	5%
0.9	0.25	75%	15%
0.5	3/4	0.4	9/10

The children may cover up 50%, 0.5 for the equivalent to ½ and 10% + 5% + 5% or 15% + 5% for totalling 20%.

Once the children have worked out the answer, they need to place their counters or pieces of paper on the appropriate squares of their grids. The winner is the first player to cover all their numbers on their grid (there are likely to be a few completing at the same time). The children need to know that sometimes they can cover more than one number, and at other times they may not be able to cover one at all.

The following pages provide sample grids and questions. Each set of questions should contain some stretching ones for the more able and some simpler ones for the lower achievers. Some of the questions will have duplicate answers in order to give the children another chance to cover the number up if they missed it the first time.

Extension

When you have played this a few times you could suggest that children make their own blank grids and fill them with their own choice of numbers. Play again with a variety of questions. Perhaps children could also work in pairs, devising their own questions for their partner.

Year 5 start of year sample questions

Use the Year 5 start of year cover up grid from photocopiable sheet 3.

1. Put counters on the amounts that are equivalent to half. (0.5, ½, ⁵⁄₁₀, ²⁄₄)
2. What is ¾ of 100? (75)
3. What fractions are the same as 0.25? (¼, ²⁄₈)
4. What fraction of 100 is 10? (¹⁄₁₀)
5. Put counters on the number that is equivalent to ¹⁄₁₀. (0.1)
6. What is ¼ of 200? (50)
7. What fraction is four out of five? (⁴⁄₅)
8. How would you write ⁶⁄₁₀ as a decimal? (0.6)
9. If I had three footballs and kicked two of them, what fraction did I kick? (²⁄₃)
10. What is ³⁄₈ and ³⁄₈? (¾)
11. What is ¹⁄₁₀ of 1000? (100)
12. What is ¹⁄₁₀ of 100? (10)

Year 5 sample questions

Use the Year 5 cover up grid from photocopiable sheet 1.

1. Put counters on the amounts that are shown that are equivalent to half. (½, ⁵⁄₁₀, 50%, 0.5)
2. What is all of something? (100%)
3. Put counters on the amounts that show one eighth. (⅛, 0.125)
4. What fraction of 100 is 70? (⁷⁄₁₀)
5. What percentage is equivalent to ¾? (75%)
6. What fraction of 200 is 120? (³⁄₅)
7. What is ½ plus ¼ plus ⅛? (⅞)
8. Which amounts are the same as 0.25? (¼, 25%.)
9. What is left if you take ⁴⁄₁₀ away from a whole? (³⁄₅)
10. How many thirds are the same as ⁸⁄₁₂? (²⁄₃)
11. 60cm is how many metres? (0.6)
12. Cover up any fractions higher than ½. (¾, ³⁄₅, ²⁄₃, ⅞, ⁷⁄₁₀)

Year 6 sample questions

Use the Year 6 cover up grid from photocopiable sheet 2.

1. Cover up amounts that show or are equivalent to ⅛. (⅛, 12½%, 0.125)
2. Cover up amounts that are equivalent to ½. (⁵⁄₁₀, ½, 0.5)
3. Cover up any amounts that are equivalent to ¼. (25%)
4. Cover up any amounts that are less than, but not including, ¼. (⅛, 12½%, 17½%, 0.125)
5. What is ¾ as a decimal? (0.75)
6. If an item in a sale was reduced by a quarter, what percentage of the original price will it be? (75%)
7. Cover up any amounts that are equivalent to 75%. (0.75, ¾, 75%)
8. What fraction of 30 is 20? (²⁄₃)
9. What is ½ plus ⅓? (⅚)
10. What is ½ plus ¼ plus ⅛? (⅞)
11. What percentage is equivalent to 0.05? (5%)
12. Cover up two or more fractions that add up to more than a whole but less than 1½. (⁴⁄₅ + ⁵⁄₁₀, ²⁄₃ + ½, ½ + ⅛ + ¾)

Photocopiable Sheet 3
Cover them up A

Year 5 start of year

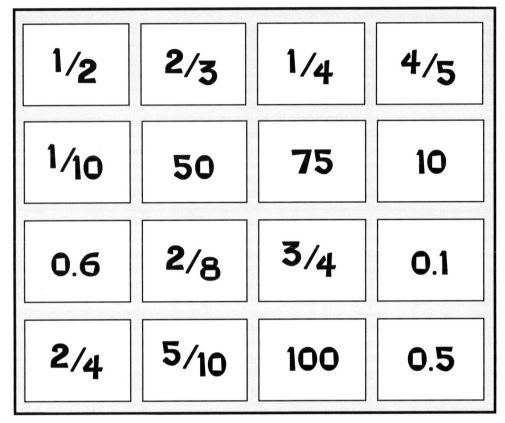

1/2	2/3	1/4	4/5
1/10	50	75	10
0.6	2/8	3/4	0.1
2/4	5/10	100	0.5

Year 5

1/2	2/3	1/4	3/5
5/10	50%	75%	25%
0.6	1/8	3/4	0.125
7/8	7/10	100%	0.5

Photocopiable Sheet 4
Cover them up B
Year 6

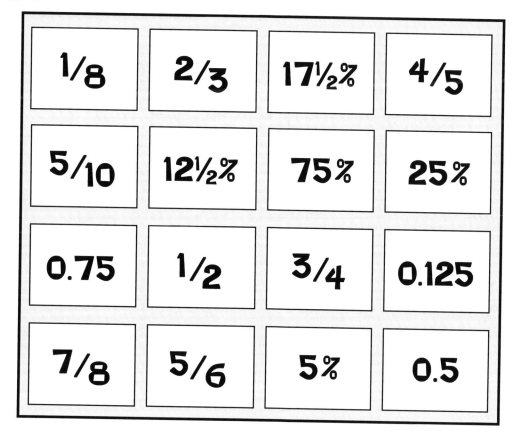

1/8	2/3	17½%	4/5
5/10	12½%	75%	25%
0.75	1/2	3/4	0.125
7/8	5/6	5%	0.5

Chapter 3

Percentage squares

This is another visual activity which is good for demonstrating links between fractions and percentages and for finding percentages of amounts of money.

Preparation
You will need:

○ an acetate copy of the percentage square, photocopiable sheet 5;

○ copies of the fraction strips, photocopiable sheets 6 and 7, photocopied onto card;

○ additional copies for use by the children.

Activities
There is enough content here for two or three lessons.

1. Display the percentage square, discuss what one square is worth, how many small squares are on the whole and therefore how many per cent make up a whole. Show the 'whole' card and cover the percentage square with it, show the 'half' card and discuss. Talk about it being half of the whole and therefore equal to half of 100%. Ask the children how many per cent this is. Repeat with the other fraction amounts – quarter, fifth, tenth, twentieth, hundredth.

2. Give the children copies of the percentage square and fractions strips. Ask them to cut the fractions out, match them to the percentage square and record, for example, ½ = 50%, ¼ = 25%, ⅕ = 20%, ⅒ = 10%, ¹⁄₂₀ = 5%, ¹⁄₁₀₀ = 1%. Then give them some more paper and ask them to investigate other fraction and percentage equivalences, for example, ⅛, ¹⁄₄₀, ¾.

3. Use the percentage square for money, for example pretend each 1% represents 5p. How much would 100% be? If something was reduced by 2%, how much would be taken off and what would it cost? If the price was increased by 8%, how much would be added on and how much would it cost? Use the percentage square for counting up the amounts. Differentiated tasks can be produced by preparing a set of questions as below and giving the children different amounts for each small percentage square.

Sample questions

1. How much does your item cost?

2. If your item was reduced in a sale by 10%, how much would be taken off?

3. How much would it cost?

4. If your item was reduced by 15%, how much would be taken off?

5. How much would it cost?

6. If your item was m price, how much would it cost?

7. If the price of your item was increased by 4%, how much more would it be?

8. How much would it cost?

9. If the price of your item was increased by 17%, how much more would it be?

10. How much would it cost?

Photocopiable Sheet 5
Percentage squares

1%	1%	1%	1%	1%	1%	1%	1%	1%	1%
1%	1%	1%	1%	1%	1%	1%	1%	1%	1%
1%	1%	1%	1%	1%	1%	1%	1%	1%	1%
1%	1%	1%	1%	1%	1%	1%	1%	1%	1%
1%	1%	1%	1%	1%	1%	1%	1%	1%	1%
1%	1%	1%	1%	1%	1%	1%	1%	1%	1%
1%	1%	1%	1%	1%	1%	1%	1%	1%	1%
1%	1%	1%	1%	1%	1%	1%	1%	1%	1%
1%	1%	1%	1%	1%	1%	1%	1%	1%	1%
1%	1%	1%	1%	1%	1%	1%	1%	1%	1%

Photocopiable Sheet 6
Fraction strips A

1 whole

Photocopiable Sheet 7
Fraction strips B

1/2

1/5

1/10

1/20

1/100

Chapter 4

Percentage game

This game for up to six players is suitable as an introduction to percentages.

Preparation
Each child needs:

O a copy of the game sheet overleaf and a copy of the percentage square from photocopiable sheet 5;

O a dice numbered 1 to 6 per group.

You will need to fill in the game sheet with a variety of percentages as shown in the example below.

Example 1

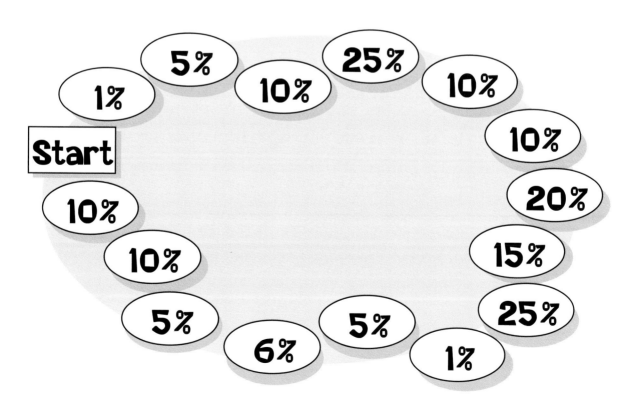

Activity

The children take it in turns to throw the dice and move around the 'course'. For each percentage they land on they need to colour in the equivalent number of squares on their percentage sheet. The winner is the child with the most squares coloured in once the course has been completed several times over a set time limit, or once they have coloured the whole square. At the end they have to land on the exact percentage to complete their square, for example, if they land on a 25% and only have 10 more squares to colour, they miss their turn.

For example, using the game sheet shown in example 1:

Player 1 throws 4, moves to fourth ellipse, colours 25% of his or her square (25 squares). Player 2 throws 2, moves to second ellipse, colours 5% of the square (five squares). Player 1 throws 6, moves on, colours 1%. So play continues.

1%	1%	1%	1%	1%	1%	1%	1%	1%	1%
1%	1%	1%	1%	1%	1%	1%	1%	1%	1%
1%	1%	1%	1%	1%	1%	1%	1%	1%	1%
1%	1%	1%	1%	1%	1%	1%	1%	1%	1%
1%	1%	1%	1%	1%	1%	1%	1%	1%	1%
1%	1%	1%	1%	1%	1%	1%	1%	1%	1%
1%	1%	1%	1%	1%	1%	1%	1%	1%	1%
1%	1%	1%	1%	1%	1%	1%	1%	1%	1%
1%	1%	1%	1%	1%	1%	1%	1%	1%	1%
1%	1%	1%	1%	1%	1%	1%	1%	1%	1%

Player 1

1%	1%	1%	1%	1%	1%	1%	1%	1%	1%
1%	1%	1%	1%	1%	1%	1%	1%	1%	1%
1%	1%	1%	1%	1%	1%	1%	1%	1%	1%
1%	1%	1%	1%	1%	1%	1%	1%	1%	1%
1%	1%	1%	1%	1%	1%	1%	1%	1%	1%
1%	1%	1%	1%	1%	1%	1%	1%	1%	1%
1%	1%	1%	1%	1%	1%	1%	1%	1%	1%
1%	1%	1%	1%	1%	1%	1%	1%	1%	1%
1%	1%	1%	1%	1%	1%	1%	1%	1%	1%
1%	1%	1%	1%	1%	1%	1%	1%	1%	1%

Player 2

Extension

As a progression, the same game can be played with fractions on the game sheet, which the children should convert to percentages and colour accordingly on their percentage square, for example:

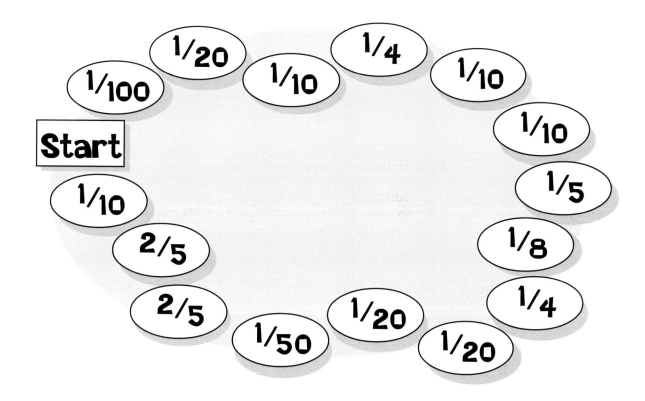

Photocopiable Sheet 8
Percentage game

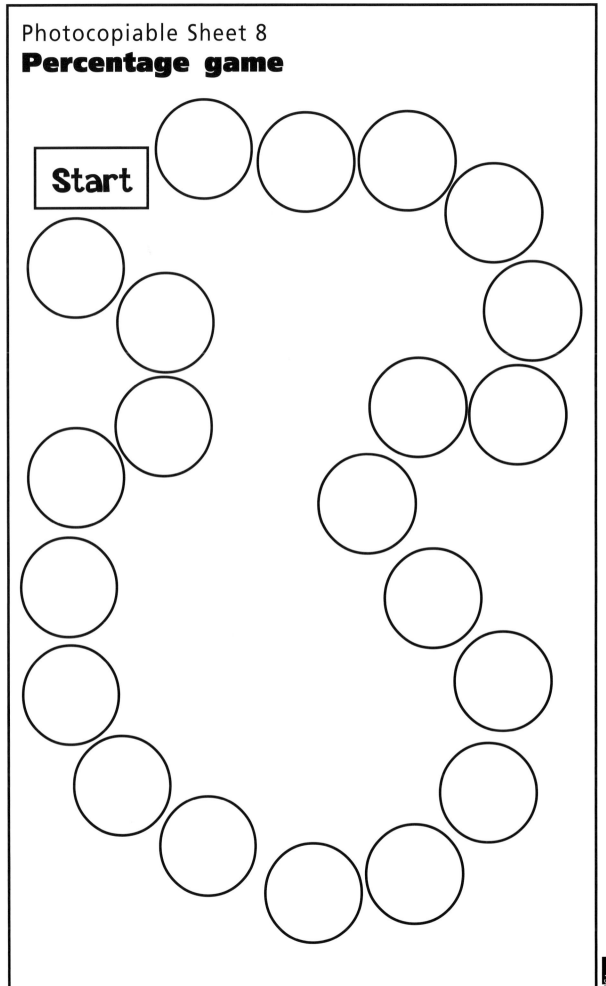

Chapter 5

Improper fractions

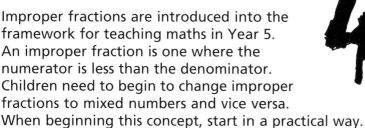

Improper fractions are introduced into the framework for teaching maths in Year 5. An improper fraction is one where the numerator is less than the denominator. Children need to begin to change improper fractions to mixed numbers and vice versa. When beginning this concept, start in a practical way.

Preparation
You will need:

O chocolate bars – or something similar that can be divided into eight;

O paper and pens for the children;

O follow-up work sheets (photocopiable sheets 9–11);

O digit cards for the children to use to generate their own numbers.

Introduction
Demonstrate by using two chocolate bars (or something similar that has eight divisions).

O Hold up one of the chocolate bars.

O Write on the board that you need $^{12}/_8$ of it.

O Ask the children to work out how you can have what you need. Hopefully they should quickly be able to tell you that you have not got enough and that you will need another chocolate bar to make it possible.

O Next work out, using the chocolate bars, how much $^{12}/_8$ actually is.

Write on the board another improper fraction, for example $^{15}/_{10}$. Convert this in the same way, discussing how many tenths make a whole and how many will be left over. Tenths are good fractions to work with as they are numerically easy to work out and enable the children to concentrate on the focus of the lesson.

After completing several examples together, write an improper fraction on the board and ask the children to record in any way that they want the mixed fraction that comes from your improper fraction. Encourage diagrams and drawings. Repeat this several times, discussing the ideas that the children have come up with.

Key questions

- Why can't I have $^{12}/_8$ of this chocolate bar?
- How many eighths make up the whole bar?
- How many more eighths do I need?
- How many eighths would there be in two bars?
- How many tenths are there in a whole?
- Can you draw a diagram to show your answer?
- Can you explain how you can make an improper fraction into a mixed number fraction?

Activities

1. The first photocopiable sheet requires the children to work out how many whole strips and how many parts have been coloured and then write that as a mixed number fraction.

2. Photocopiable sheets 2 and 3, which could be used as a follow up, require the children to colour the improper fractions on the strips or shapes and convert them into mixed number fractions. They then make up their own shapes.

3. Another idea is to ask the children to use their digit cards to generate their own improper fractions as follows:

Pick three digit cards, use two as the numerator and the third as the denominator, for example:

Ask the children to write their improper fraction on a piece of paper and work out what it would be as a mixed number.

For the lower achieving children in your class, ask them to do the same thing using two digit cards, making the higher one the numerator, for example:

Photocopiable Sheet 9
Improper fractions A

How many whole strips and parts have been coloured?

Example

$$2^{1/4}$$

© The Questions Publishing Company Ltd

Photocopiable Sheet 10
Improper fractions B

Colour these shapes in to show the improper fraction.

Example

7/3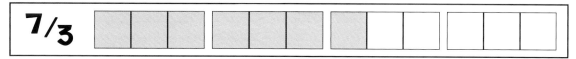

11/3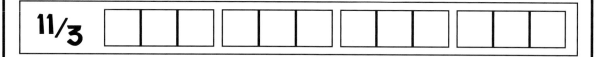

9/3

5/3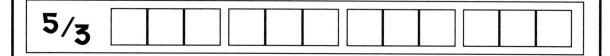

7/4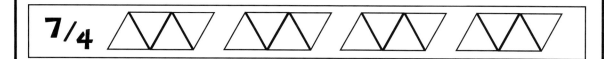

11/4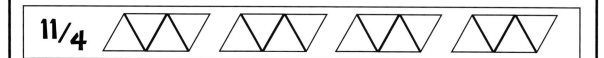

13/4

16/4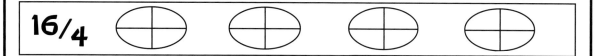

Photocopiable Sheet 11
Improper fractions C

Now draw your own shapes for these fractions and write the mixed number fraction.

12/5

Mixed number fraction: _____

14/5

Mixed number fraction: _____

8/5

Mixed number fraction: _____

17/5

Mixed number fraction: _____

9/6

Mixed number fraction: _____

14/6

Mixed number fraction: _____

13/10

Mixed number fraction: _____

22/10

Mixed number fraction: _____

Chapter 6

Fractions to decimals

The children need to be able to enter fractions into a calculator and interpret the display to find the equivalent decimal. They also need to be able to predict the result before confirming. This activity will be a helpful starting point.

Preparation
You will need:

○ one calculator per child plus, if possible an OHP calculator for use by you with OHP.

○ photocopiable sheet 12, one per child/pair/group.

○ digit cards.

Starting activity
Introduce the activity by talking about simple fractions such as a half and a quarter. Discuss what a half is (one thing divided into two). Ask the children what that would be as a decimal. They should have this prior knowledge from work done in Year 4.

Discuss other fractions, for example, ⅓, ⅕. What are they? (One thing divided by 3 or 5.) How can we find out what they are as decimals using a calculator? Divide one by three or five. Ask the children to work this out. ⅓ will become 0.333333333. Round that to the nearest hundredth to make 0.33. ⅕ will become 0.2. Ask them to try ⅔, ⅗, predicting first.

Give the children a piece of spare paper each. Call out some fractions and ask them to predict what each one will be as a decimal, for example:

Year 5: ¼, ¾, ¹⁄₁₀, ¹⁄₁₀₀, ⁵⁰⁄₁₀₀

Year 6: ¹⁄₁₀₀₀, ⅛, ⅔

Check together using calculators. Round ⅔ to the nearest hundredth.

Follow-up activities

1. Brainstorm some fractions together on the board – about 20. Ask the children to choose between six and ten, suggesting that certain children should tackle certain fractions (depending on ability). Give them a copy of the photocopiable sheet 12. Ask them to predict what their fractions will be as decimals, check using a calculator and then draw a number line and plot them onto it as both fractions and decimals, as shown below.

Fraction	Prediction	Actual
½	0.5	0.5
⅗	0.6	0.6
⅚	0.9	0.83
⁷⁄₁₀	0.7	0.7
⁴⁄₉	0.99	0.44
⅝	0.6	0.625

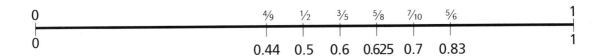

2. The children will need a set of digit cards each. Ask them to make up their own fractions by picking two or three (for the more able) cards and arranging them into a proper fraction, e.g. they pick four and seven and make ⁴⁄₇, predict the decimal equivalent and plot on a number line as in activity 1.

3. Ask the children to find as many fractions as they can between ½ and ¾, by investigating as many numbers as possible through turning them into decimals and order, for example:

Year 5
Concentrate on thirds, fifths and tenths:

Would ⅔ come between ½ and ¾? What about ⅓, ⅖ and ⅗ and so on.

Year 6
Concentrate on sixths, eighths and twelfths and for more able children add in sevenths and ninths:

Would ⁴⁄₇ come between ½ and ¾? What about ⁵⁄₇, ⁷⁄₁₂ , ⁸⁄₉ and so on.

The amount you would expect them to find will vary according to year group and ability. Have a competition between the groups to see who can find the most.

Photocopiable Sheet 12
Fractions to decimals

Fraction	Prediction	Actual

0   1

0   1

0   1

0   1

Chapter 7

Paint ratios

This is an extremely practical way to introduce ratio to Year 6 children.

Preparation
You will need:

O two colours of OHP counters and/or two different shapes;

O OHP;

O red and yellow paints;

O brushes;

O spoons;

O copy of photocopiable sheet 13, page 31, for each group of children.

Whole-class starting activity
Explain the concept of ratio: that it is one part of something to another part of something else.

Use ten OHP counters of two different colours, and ten shapes of two different types, and an OHP to make this clear.

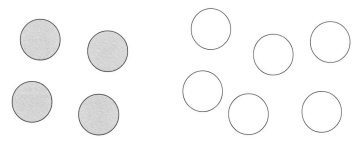

Explain that there are ten counters. Four are green and six are blue. For every four green counters there are six blue ones. This is a ratio and can be written 4:6.

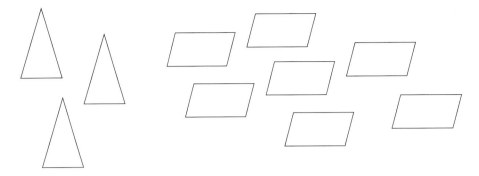

Explain that there are ten shapes. Three are triangles and seven are parallelograms. For every three triangles there are seven parallelograms. This is a ratio and can be written 3:7.

Repeat this with different numbers of counters and shapes, questioning the children.

Key questions

- How many green counters now?
- How many blue?
- For every x number of blue counters, how many are green?
- What is the ratio?

Explain how useful ratio is by referring to familiar experiences, for example when mixing drinks. Demonstrate using squash. Make up a drink with one tablespoon of cordial and eight tablespoons of water. Explain the ratio is 1:8, i.e. one part cordial for every eight of water.

Another example is making powder paint. Demonstrate by making different consistencies. Involve the children in doing this. Use one scoop of red powder and four of water, one scoop of powder and six scoops of water. Do this several times, explaining the ratio as before. Brush the paint on paper so that the children can see the effect of the different ratios. Ask if they can explain why knowing about ratio is important.

Move on to the follow-up activity, which is a version of the paint demonstration you have performed.

Follow-up activity

Give the children access to some red and yellow paints, paintbrushes, spoons and the paint ratio sheet. They will need to be able to work in mixed ability groups of three to five. As a group they need to decide which child will mix the paints to which ratio, for example Gemma may mix the paints to a ratio of one spoon of red to two of yellow; Adam might choose two of red to one of yellow. After each child has decided and mixed their paint, they need to make a splodge of it on their activity sheet and label the ratio. After this, encourage the children to look at each other's splodges and order the shades from lightest to darkest. Ask the children to be prepared to show the others what they have done during the plenary session.

During the plenary ask selected groups to show their splodges. Ask the rest of the class to order their paintings and guess what ratios they had used. Order the ratios on a number line on the board from lightest to darkest.

Photocopiable Sheet 13
Paint blots

My paint ratio is:

Chapter 8

Map reading

Another effective way of teaching ratio is through map reading. This activity is suitable for Year 6 children.

Preparation
You will need for each child:

O a selection of maps or atlases with scales;

O photocopiable sheet 14;

O string;

O ruler.

Starting activity
Give the children maps or atlases and ask them to look for the scales. Ask for examples, pick a few to discuss. One child might say, for example, 'The scale I've found says 1cm:10km.' Ask the children what they think that means. In this particular instance, every 1cm measured represents 10 real kilometres. Ask them to work out what the real distance would be if it measured 3cm from one place to another, 7cm, 2.5cm and so on.

Ask the children to measure some distances from one place to another on their maps 'as the crow flies'. Take feedback.

Follow-up activities

1. Give children a copy of a map of an area that they are studying in a geography topic, with a simple scale, for example, 1cm:10km, some string and a ruler. Ask them to use the string to measure distances along the shortest road routes from one place to another. Lay the string along the ruler, find its length in centimetres and convert it to kilometres to find the real distance. Take feedback.

2. Repeat the above activity using an imaginary map such as that below, which can be copied from photocopiable sheet 14 for the children.

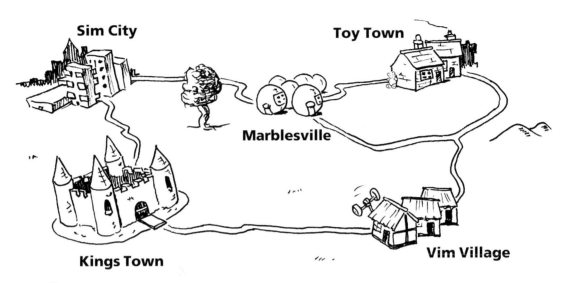

Sim City

Toy Town

Marblesville

Kings Town

Vim Village

1cm = 10km

Key questions

○ How far is it from Marblesville to Vim Village by the most direct route?
○ How far is it from Toy Town to Kings Town via Vim Village?
○ How far would it be to go to all the places by the shortest routes?
○ How far is it from Sim City to Marblesville and back?

3. Ask the children to draw their own map, with four or five imaginary places. Ask them to make up a scale of a realistic ratio and work out the distances from one place to another. Ask them to make up some questions about their map for a friend to answer.

Photocopiable Sheet 14
Map reading

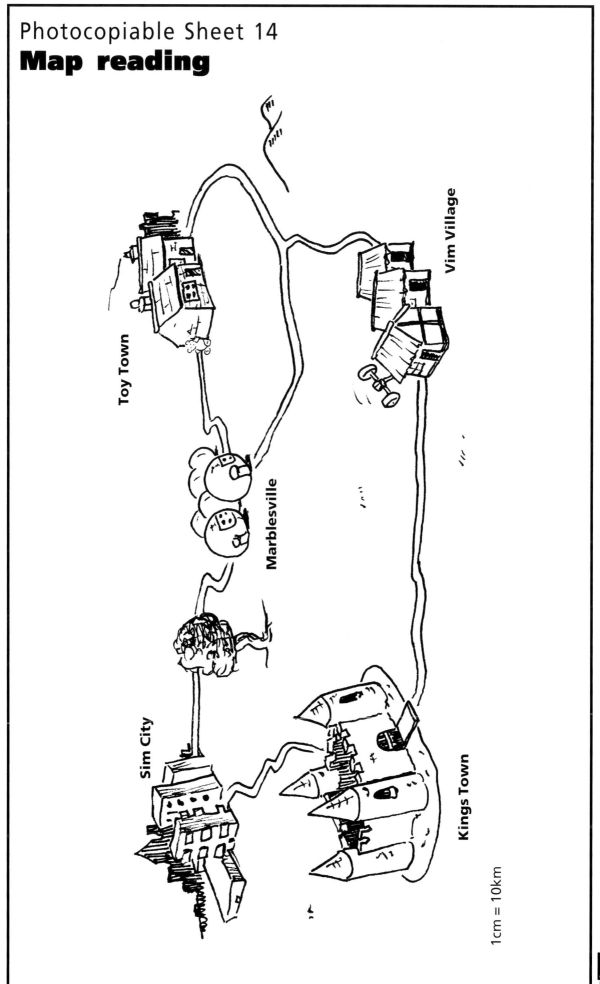

Toy Town

Vim Village

Marblesville

Sim City

Kings Town

1cm = 10km

Chapter 9

Ratios and heights

Reinforce the usefulness of ratio by looking at heights of objects and working out a ratio, so that they can be represented on paper.

Preparation
You will need:

O photograph of a child or a picture;

O tape measures or meter sticks and rulers;

O A3 paper;

O a variety of objects from the classroom to be available for the children to use;

O rulers;

O paper;

O photocopiable sheets 15–17.

Starting activity
Show a picture of a child, preferably a photograph. Ask the children what the difference is between the picture and a real child. Expect all kinds of answers. Accept them but lead towards the size aspect. Explain that the child is in proportion but is smaller in the photograph. Ask them what has been done to make him or her smaller.

Choose some children to help you. Tell the class that you want to make a drawing of each child, to show how tall he or she is. But you only have a piece of A3 paper. Ask for suggestions of how to do this. Hopefully someone may suggest something similar to this: for every 10cm tall that they are, draw 1cm. Make the suggestion yourself if necessary. Measure your helpers, write their heights on the board and convert them to a ratio of 1cm for every 10cm, so if one of your helpers is 1m 45cm tall, their representation on paper will be 14.5cm.

Ask some children to draw the heights you have converted and order from tallest to shortest. Do the same with the children and see if the two are comparable.

Follow-up activities

Year 5:

This would be best done in pairs, but you may prefer to ask the children to work in groups or individually. Ask the children to select ten objects, measure them accurately, convert them to a smaller height using the ratio of 1cm:10cm, and then draw a line to that conversion. Use the table on photocopiable sheet 1 to complete their investigation.

Year 5 and 6:

Complete photocopiable sheet 16, which is converting heights of building to a ratio of 1cm:10m and drawing them.

Year 6:

Complete photocopiable sheet 17, which is similar to the second but involves converting to ratios of 1cm:10m and 1cm:100m and comparing the results.

Photocopiable Sheet 15
Ratios and heights 1

Use this sheet to help you with your ratio work.

Object	Height	Ratio of 1cm:10cm

Draw a line to show the height of your object at a ratio of 1cm:10cm

Photocopiable Sheet 16
Ratios and heights 2

Work out the measurements of these buildings in centimetres at a ratio of 1cm for every 10m.

Object	Height	Ratio of 1cm:10m
St Paul's Cathedral	111m	
Big Ben	97m	
London Hilton	100m	
Blackpool Tower	158m	
Empire State Building	381m	
Bank of Manhattan	274m	
Fawley Power Station	198m	
Canary Wharf	244m	

Draw lines in centimetres to represent the heights of the buildings at a ratio of 1cm:10m. Some of them will not fit on this page.
Use a large piece of paper.

Photocopiable Sheet 17
Ratios and heights 3

Work out the measurements of these buildings in centimetres at a ratio of 1cm for every 10m and 1cm for every 100m.

Object	Height	Ratio of 1cm:10m	Ratio of 1cm:100m
St Paul's Cathedral	111m		
Big Ben	97m		
London Hilton	100m		
Blackpool Tower	158m		
Empire State Building	381m		
Bank of Manhattan	274m		
Fawley Power Station	198m		
Canary Wharf	244m		

Draw lines in centimetres to represent the heights of the buildings at a ratio of 1cm:100cm.

Chapter 10

My body

This activity, suitable for Year 6, combines ratio, proportion and some fraction work. It involves working in pairs and measuring. To be taught effectively, this activity will probably need two or three days to complete.

Preparation
You will need:

O two different colours of OHP counters or two different shapes;

O a doll;

O strips of paper;

O glue.

Starting activity
Discuss the words ratio and proportion. What do they mean? Ratio is one for every, and proportion is one out of every. Demonstrate this using two colours of OHP counters or two different shapes on the OHP as follows:

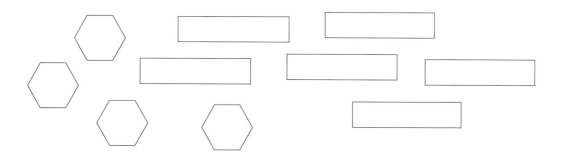

There are ten shapes. Four of them are hexagons and six are oblongs. The ratio is 4:6 because for every four hexagons there are six oblongs. If there were 20 shapes in this ratio, how many hexagons would there be? Oblongs? If there were 30 shapes, how many hexagons? Oblongs?

The proportion of hexagons is four out of ten because there are 10 shapes altogether and four of them are hexagons. This can be written as a fraction. The proportion of oblongs is what?

Demonstrate several times using different combinations of ten coloured counters or shapes. Ask the children to come to the OHP and help you, giving their own suggestions.

Demonstrate the idea of ratio and proportion again using a doll. Have prepared several strips of paper: one the length of the doll's head; one of its height and one of the length of the rest of its body (minus head).

Measure the doll's height, the length of its head from the crown to the chin and work out from those the rest of its body, for example, height 36cm, length of head 12cm, rest of body 24cm. Discuss this in terms of ratio and proportion, i.e. the ratio is 12cm:24cm, or, if reduced, 1:2, because for every 12cm of head there is 24cm of the rest of the body.

Demonstrate using the head strips and rest of body strips of paper that you prepared earlier.

Discuss what the size of the doll's body would be if its head were 24cm long.

The proportion is 12cm out of 36cm, or $^{12}/_{36}$, or $^1/_3$ because the head is 12cms out of the whole height of 36cm, which, reduced, makes one out of three. This is quite a confusing idea, so you will need to demonstrate by using the strips of paper the length of the doll and the length of its head. Show that three head pieces make the whole doll, so the head is $^1/_3$ of the whole doll. The proportion of body to doll is 24cm out of 36cm, which can be reduced to $^2/_3$.

Now demonstrate using a child – the measurements and proportions will be very different.

Height:	154cm
Head:	22cm
Therefore the rest of body:	132cm

Work out the ratio of head to body with the children, i.e. 22cm:132cm because for every 22cm head there is 132cm of body. Ask if this can be reduced. It can be reduced to 1:6 by dividing, for example, by 11 and then two. To make this even clearer cut a strip of paper to the length of the child's head – 22cm.

Work out how many heads fit the length of the body. If the measurements are not completely accurate, approximate your answer.

In this case it is seven. Now show that one head fits into the body part 6 times. Work out the proportion in a similar way, i.e. 22cm out of 154cm is head, so the proportion of head is $^{22}/_{154}$, or when reduced, one out of seven or $^1/_7$. The proportion of body is 132cm out of 154cm or $^{132}/_{154}$ or $^6/_7$.

Again demonstrate using the strips of paper you prepared.

Activity

The children need to work in pairs. Give them the appropriate measuring equipment to choose from, paper for cutting into strips and paper to work on. Their task is to work out as accurately as possible the ratio of their partner's head to the rest of his or her body, and the proportions of both. They need to have a result in centimetres as well as a reduced ratio and proportion fraction. It would be clearer for the children to fill in a table as shown below.

	Head	**Body**
Measurement (cm)	12	84
Ratio	1:7	7:1
Proportion	⅛	⅞

Afterwards, get together as a group and discuss what they have done and whether any conclusion can be made. Hopefully most of their work will indicate that all these body parts are of the same ratio and proportion regardless of their size.

Follow-up activities

1. Similar investigations can be carried out with other parts of the body, for example, foot and arm (from shoulder to wrist), hand to arm.

2. Ask the children to experiment with their own body part ideas.